BODY

Andrew Haslam

written by
Liz Wyse

Photography by Jon Barnes

A **TWO-CAN** BOOK
published by
THOMSON LEARNING
New York

MAKE it WORK!
Other titles

Building
Insects
Machines

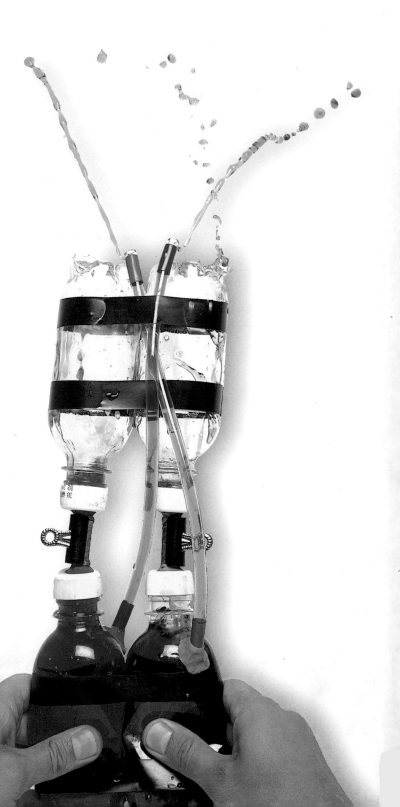

First published in the United States in 1994 by
Thomson Learning
115 Fifth Avenue
New York, NY 10003

First published in Great Britain in 1994 by
Two-Can Publishing Ltd.

Printed and bound in Hong Kong

Library of Congress Cataloging-in-Publication Data

Haslam, Andrew
Body/Andrew Haslam; written by Liz Wyse; photography, Jon Barnes.
  p. cm. – (Make it work!)
"A Two-Can book."
Includes bibliographical references and index.
ISBN: 1-56847-258-7
1. Human anatomy – Juvenile literature. [1.Body, Human – Experiments. 2. Human physiology – Experiments.
3. Experiments. 4. Scientific recreations.] I. Wyse Liz. II. Barnes, Jon, ill. III. Title. IV. Series: Baker, Wendy. Make-it-work!
QM27.H37 1994
611–dc20   94-1479

Editor: Lucy Duke
Series concept and original design: Andrew Haslam and Wendy Baker
Assistant model-maker: Sarah Davies
Additional design: Lisa Nutt

Thanks also to:
Colin and Jenny at Plough Studios.

Contents

Words that appear in **bold** in the text
are explained in the glossary.

Did you know that your body contains more than 200 bones and 600 muscles, or that your heart beats 100,000 times a day and never rests? Do you realize that your body is about 70 percent water? The human body is a fascinating world just waiting to be explored.

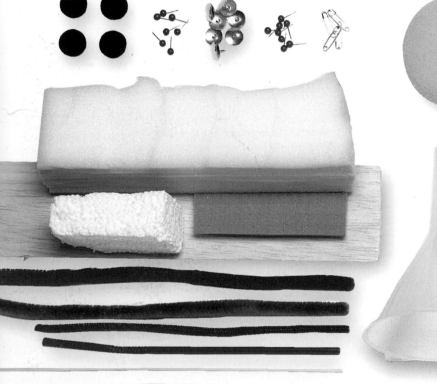

*All human beings belong to a **species**, or group, called Homo sapiens, or "wise man."*

Biologists are scientists who examine the living world. All living things, including human beings, share certain characteristics. They take in food and use the chemical energy they obtain from it to help them grow and move. They make waste products. They respond to the world around them. They all start out as a single **cell**, and reproduce to create new life.

What are humans?

Human beings belong to the big group of animals called mammals. We share a number of important characteristics with other mammals. We have a bony skeleton, which is inside our body. We are warm-blooded, which means that our body controls its own temperature. And we give birth to live young, and feed our babies on milk made inside the mother's body.

A crafty tip

To paint your body models, use acrylic paint or mix ordinary paint with rubber cement.

MAKE it WORK!

Become a human biologist. Take a closer look at yourself and the people around you. You can try the experiments in this book on yourself or your friends. Many of the activities will show you the world that lies beneath your skin, so you can find out what happens under the surface. There are also models to make that will help you to understand how important **organs**, such as your heart and lungs, actually work.

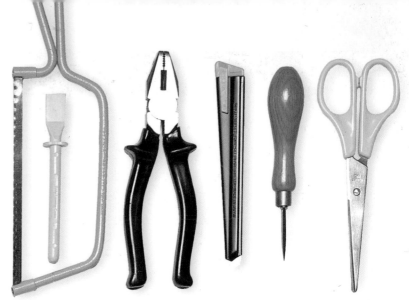

Modeling the body

You will be making life-size models of all the body's main systems. Eventually, you will see your own body "inside out"! The pictures show you some of the equipment you will need.

Doing experiments

Several experiments will show you how your body works. As a scientist, you must be careful to keep a record of all your experiments. You can do this by writing notes, or you could record your findings on a tape recorder. The main equipment and tools you will need for your experiments are shown in the picture.

Did you know you are the end result of up to 1¹/₂ million years of human history? In this time, humans have changed and developed. We have learned to walk upright and use our hands to work with tools. We have also learned to use language to communicate with one another.

Your **skeleton** is your body's framework. It is made up of 206 bones, which meet and link up at **joints**. Your bones come in many different sizes and shapes, depending on the jobs they have to do. The largest bone in the human body is the thigh bone, or femur. The smallest is a tiny bone inside the ear called the stirrup.

Standing up straight

Most mammals move along on all fours. Our human skeleton, helped by our **muscles** and **ligaments**, allows us to walk around while still standing up straight. The long, thick bones of our legs and feet carry the weight of our bodies. The bowl-shaped bones of the pelvis (or hips) are a firm base for the spine (or backbone).

MAKE it WORK!

Have you ever wondered what it would be like to see through your skin and muscles to the skeleton underneath? Make your own bones from cut-out cardboard, stick them in position, and turn yourself into a real live skeleton!

You will need

a pair of scissors
double-sided tape
paints or colored pencils
sheets of light-colored cardboard

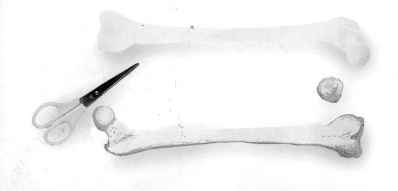

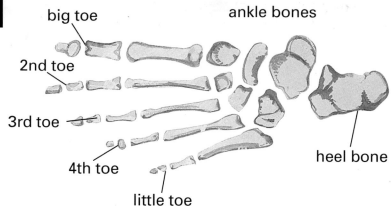

big toe   ankle bones
2nd toe
3rd toe
4th toe
little toe
heel bone

▲ Humans have short, stiff toes that give us a strong, springy base, pushing the body off the ground as we walk along and helping us to keep our balance.

calf bone   shin bone

ankle bones
toe bones   foot bones   kneecap   thigh bone

1 Following the photographs above, draw all the bone shapes on the cardboard. Try to measure them to fit your body.

2 Cut out the bone shapes.

3 Use paints or pencils to color the bones – make them darker around the joints (where two bones meet).

The protecting skeleton

Some bones protect the organs inside our bodies. The rounded shape of the pelvis guards the bladder. Ribs surround the heart and lungs like the curved bars of a cage, and the skull protects the brain.

All mammals have more or less the same number of bones in their bodies, whatever their size. A mouse has just as many bones as an elephant.

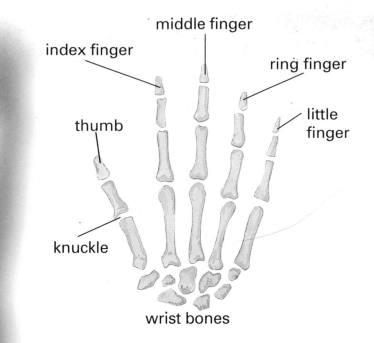

index finger
middle finger
ring finger
thumb
little finger
knuckle
wrist bones

▲ Humans have extra-long, flexible thumbs, which are able to touch each fingertip. Long thumbs enable our hands to grip large objects, as well as to carry out more delicate jobs such as threading needles.

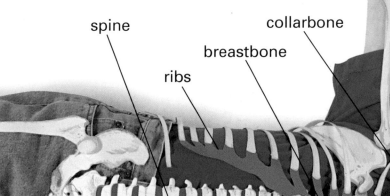

spine
collarbone
breastbone
ribs
pelvis (hip bone)
shoulder blade
upper arm bone
forearm bones

4 Put on some old, solid-colored clothes. Then ask a friend to help you stick the skeleton to your body using double-sided tape.

5 When you come to the bones of the upper body, tape the spine and shoulder blades on first. The ribs fit in a curve around the spine.

Living bones

Did you know that bones are actually alive? If they are cracked or broken they can mend themselves. They simply make new bone **tissue** that knits together the gap made by the break.

*The hard outer case of a bone surrounds a spongy inside. Some bones also contain a jellylike substance called **marrow**. Bone marrow is vitally important for a healthy body because it makes new red blood cells.*

Your skull is a hard case made of bone that protects your brain and your sense organs. Eight strong, bony plates at the top of your skull are joined together, curving around your brain. The bones of your lower skull protect your eyes and ears. Your teeth are set firmly in small holes in your upper and lower jawbones.

A crafty tip For some activities in this book, you will need to cut out difficult cardboard shapes. If anyone has a photocopier you can use, you could copy the shapes onto tracing paper, enlarge them on the photocopier, then cut out the photocopies to make full-size templates.

1 Cut out the skull shape from the cardboard.

2 Copy the wavy lines shown in the photograph. These lines on the skull are called sutures. They show where the bones have fused together.

You will need
scissors   glue
a large piece of thin cardboard
two paper fasteners

MAKE it WORK!
Make your own cardboard skull, complete with hinged jawbone, and see for yourself exactly how the fused bones of the upper skull fit together. The jawbone is the only part of the skull with joints that can actually move.

When you were born, your skull was soft because the bones were still forming. By the time you were two, the separate bones had hardened and knitted together. The lines where they joined are visible on the skull. As you get older, these lines begin to fade and may disappear altogether.

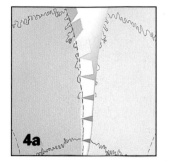

4a

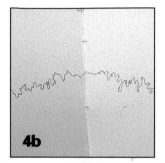

4b

5 Join the jawbone to either side of the skull using the two paper fasteners.

6 Finally, glue all thirty-two teeth in place, one set on the upper jaw and one on the lower jaw. You should now have a grinning skull!

3 Cut along the solid lines to make tabs. Score and fold along the dotted lines.

4 Glue the tabs along the top and sides of the skull.

ear canal
leads inward to the inner ear

eyeballs
protected by the eye sockets

teeth

hinged joint
attaches the jawbone to the skull

jawbone

There are 22 bones in your skull, and 14 of these are in your face. Your nose and your ears are not made of bone, so they are not part of your skull. They are made of softer, flexible tissue called cartilage, which gives them their shape.

Where two bones meet, they form a joint. Our joints let us bend, twist, and turn our bodies. At the joint, the bones are cushioned from each other by soft, protective tissue called cartilage, and also by a special fluid that prevents them from grinding against each other. Ligaments act like stretchy straps to hold the bones together.

You will need

Styrofoam blocks felt-tip pens
acrylic paint a craft file

1 Draw the shapes of the joints on the Styrofoam as shown. Use a craft file to carve them out, using the lines as guides.

2 Paint the finished joints creamy yellow.

Fused joints The joints of your skull are fused together, like the pieces of a jigsaw. They form a solid bony plate, which protects your brain.

axis

atlas

skull

MAKE it WORK!

You have many types of joints in your body. Each is specially designed for different kinds of movement. Joints help you to hold your head up, walk, and use your hands and fingers in many different ways. Make these models to find out how the joint matches the movement.

Cartilaginous joints Your spine has 24 bones. The joints between them are called cartilaginous joints. They allow your spine to be flexible.

◀ **Pivot joints** In your neck you have a pivot joint, which lets you nod and shake your head. The atlas bone rotates around the axis bone at the top of your spine to make this special joint.

Look at your own body and see how your joints work. It is easy to see, for example, that your elbow has a hinge joint. Compare the range of movement in your elbow with your shoulder, which has a different, more flexible joint.

An average person
flexes the finger joints
25 million times in his or her life!
Not surprisingly, the joints can wear out.
They become swollen and painful. This is called osteoarthritis.

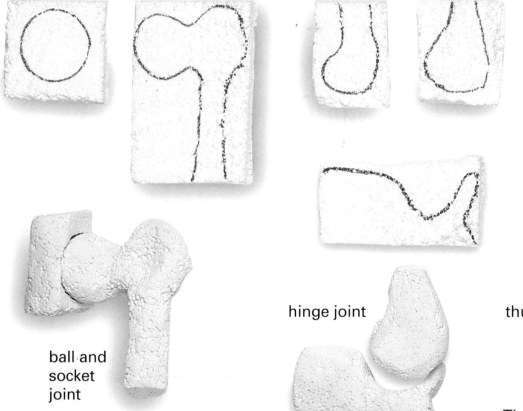

hinge joint

thumb joint

ball and socket joint

Ball and socket joints The end of one bone is ball-shaped and swivels around in the cup-shaped socket bone. Ball and socket joints are found in your hips and shoulders. Very supple people have a great range of movement in these joints.

Hinge joints These joints move back and forth in a straight line, like the hinges on a door. You will find this kind of joint in your elbows and knees.

Thumb joints The lowest bone in your thumb (the **metacarpal**) has a little lip at the end. This slots neatly into the small bone at the base of your thumb. When these two bones work together they give your thumb complete circular movement.

12 Muscles

The bones of the skeleton are moved by muscles. The human body has about 600 **skeletal** muscles. These move because you decide they should. Other **involuntary** muscles, such as those in your digestive system, move when your body needs them to work.

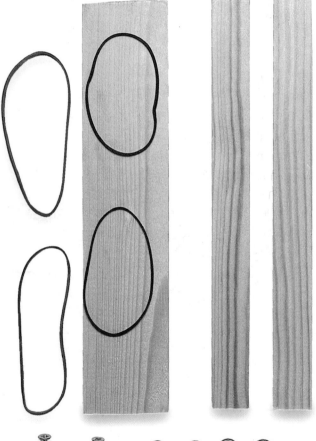

You will need

a hinge
a screwdriver
three strips of wood
two red and two green rubber bands
four screws
seven open hooks
two closed hooks

MAKE it WORK!

Muscles are joined to bones by **tendons**, which are like strips of elastic. They work by pulling against the bone to which they are attached. Make your own working muscle model and see for yourself how strong your muscles have to be.

1 Use the screwdriver to screw the hinge onto one end of the wider piece of wood. Screw the two narrower pieces to the other half of the hinge. The pieces of wood represent the three bones of your arm. You can compare them with the arm bones you made on page 7.

2 Twist four of the open hooks and one closed hook into the wood as shown. Thread the red rubber bands through the closed hook and stretch them between the open hooks. These bands represent the biceps, which is the muscle inside your upper arm.

3 Screw in the remaining hooks as shown and attach green rubber bands to form the triceps, the muscle on the outside of your upper arm.

Your completed working model shows you how muscles often work in pairs (represented by the different-colored bands). One muscle contracts, or gets shorter and fatter. As it shortens, it pulls the bone it is attached to, bending the joint. The other muscle in the pair works in the same way to straighten the joint out. Muscles need to work together like this so that joints don't get stuck in one position.

Walking may seem simple, but did you know that this action uses 200 muscles?

Ligaments hold bones together at the joint. They also keep joints from being moved too far in one direction. You can use a protractor to measure the range of movement in various joints in your body, such as your arm, knee, or thumb. You will find that some people have a much wider range of movement than others. Exercising muscles can increase their range. Ballet dancers, for example, train their bodies to become very flexible.

The human body contains more than 600 muscles. In adults, muscles make up nearly half the body weight.

If muscles are overworked, they can stay contracted for too long. This is called a cramp.

Your skin is your largest organ, covering the whole of your body – even the inside of body openings such as your mouth and nose. Your skin is waterproof. It also protects your body from infections, injuries, and the sun's harmful rays. The top layer of your skin consists of dead cells. Underneath, there are millions of tiny living cells. Each cell lives for about three weeks. As it grows older, it rises to the top of your skin and is rubbed off and replaced.

MAKE it WORK!

Make a model that will show you what goes on beneath your skin. Your skin not only protects your body, but also helps to control its temperature. Sweat **glands** pass sweat onto the surface of your skin. The sweat then **evaporates**, helping you to cool down.

You will need

dowels
a craft file
a felt-tip pen
blue, red, and white wire

a Styrofoam block
acrylic paint

1 Draw the rough shape of the skin cross section on the block of Styrofoam. Carefully carve out the shape using a craft file.

2 Shape the surface of the skin as shown. The hollows are the **pores**, which is where the sweat passes out.

3 Shape the layers of the skin as shown. You will see that there are three main layers. Carve the side of the cross section to make the three-dimensional shape of the sweat glands and hair **follicles**. The hairs on your body all grow out of follicles like these, buried under the top layers of your skin.

4 Push the dowels into the surface of the skin model. These represent the hairs that cover the entire surface of your body (except for the palms of your hands and soles of your feet).

5 Paint your model, using the different colors shown to represent the muscles, fatty tissue, sweat glands, and hair follicles.

Fingerprints are patterns on your skin's lower layer, the dermis. No two people, not even twins, have the same fingerprints.

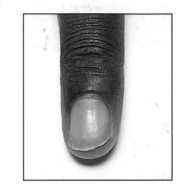 

epidermis
the outer layer of the skin

hair

pore

sebaceous gland
supplies oil to the hair

All kinds of skin

The skin on your lips is very thin, while the skin on the soles of your feet is thick and tough. Your nails are made of a hard substance called keratin, produced by cells in your skin. Your skin's cells also make melanin to protect it from the sun. The more melanin your body makes to protect you from harmful rays, the darker your skin.

muscle

hair root

sweat gland

hair follicle

fatty tissue

6 Twist red wires (representing blood-carrying capillaries) firmly into the model. Add the blue wires to represent the veins. Finally, add the white wires. These are the nerve endings which lie just below the surface of the skin.

You have about 100,000 hairs on your head. Each hair is made of tough keratin (like your nails) and can keep growing for six years.

Cells are the building blocks of the human body. Every part of your body – bones, skin, nerves, muscles – is made of cells. Although cells that do different jobs have different shapes and sizes, their basic structure is always the same.

Every single cell has its own control center, or nucleus. This contains, in **chromosomes,** the instructions that the cell needs to keep on working.

▲ Humans belong to one big interrelated group. They may not look related – they have different-colored skin, hair, and eyes. But they all belong to one species, or biological unit.

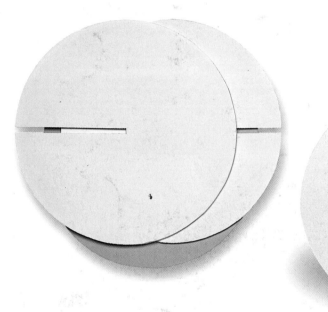

2 Cut a slot from the edge of each cardboard circle to its center. Make the slot as wide as the thickness of the cardboard.

3 Slot the two cardboard circles together as shown, and glue them into place. Paint them yellow.

4 Fold the paper circles in half, and glue them to the inside faces of your cardboard cell.

MAKE it WORK!
Make a model cross section of a cell and see for yourself the complicated world it contains. There are about 50 billion cells in your body.

You will need
strong florist's wire
thick cardboard
modeling clay
acrylic paint

electrical wire
mapping pins
yellow paper
a foam ball

1 Cut two circles out of the cardboard. Then cut four matching circles out of the yellow paper.

5 Use the foam ball to make the cell nucleus. Paint the outside of the ball green, then cut out a quarter-segment.

6 Glue the ball to the wall of the cell as shown and paint the center of the nucleus blue.

lysosome — destroys harmful substances

mitochondrion — the cell's energy store

cytoplasm — liquid containing chemicals needed to keep the cell alive; holds the floating parts of the cell together

ribosome — makes chemical substances used in the cell and elsewhere in the body

nucleus — the control center; contains instructions to keep the cell working

membrane — the thin cell wall; through this membrane, oxygen and food products enter and waste products are taken away

Golgi bodies — the cell's transportation system

7 With the modeling clay, shape all the other parts of the cell, using the photograph as a guide. Paint them. Push the pieces of electrical wire and mapping pins into the cardboard.

8 Use the strong florist's wire to attach some of the floating parts of the cell to its walls. Glue the other parts directly onto the cardboard surface.

Most cells can reproduce themselves and will do so throughout your life. Some cells can live for only a few hours, days, or weeks, but others last longer. Bone cells live for up to 20 years, while skin cells live for only three weeks. Your nerve cells cannot reproduce, so they have to last all your life.

Millions of nerves make up your body's communication system. They carry electrical messages to and from your brain. Your brain and spinal cord operate the main organs of your body without your having to think about it. Your **sense** organs send messages to your brain about the outside world (see pages 36 to 41).

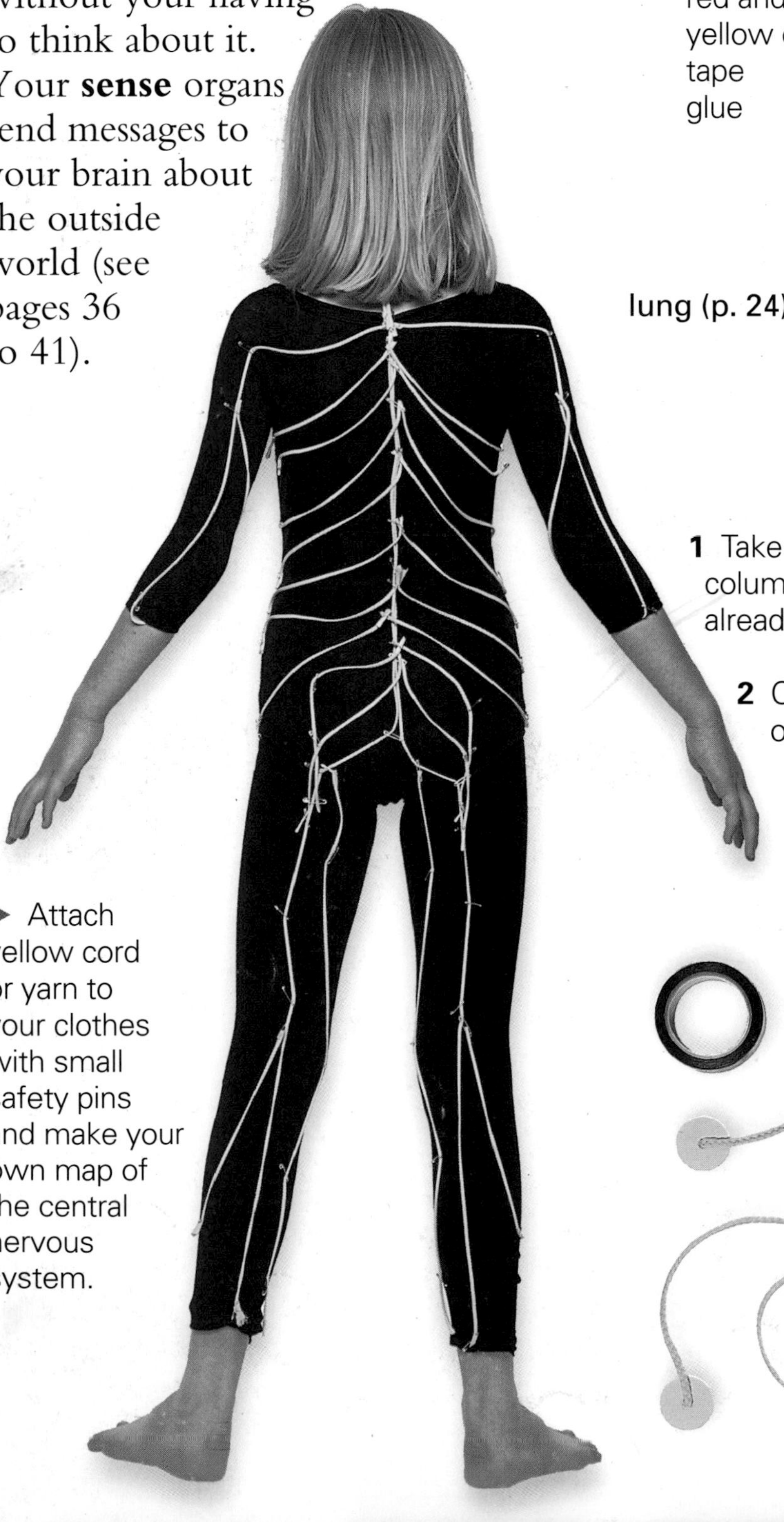

▶ Attach yellow cord or yarn to your clothes with small safety pins and make your own map of the central nervous system.

MAKE it WORK!

Make a model of the nervous system. You will see how nerves from the main organs of the body are linked to the spinal cord. The spine sends messages directly back and forth between the body and the brain.

You will need
red and yellow paper
yellow cord
tape
glue

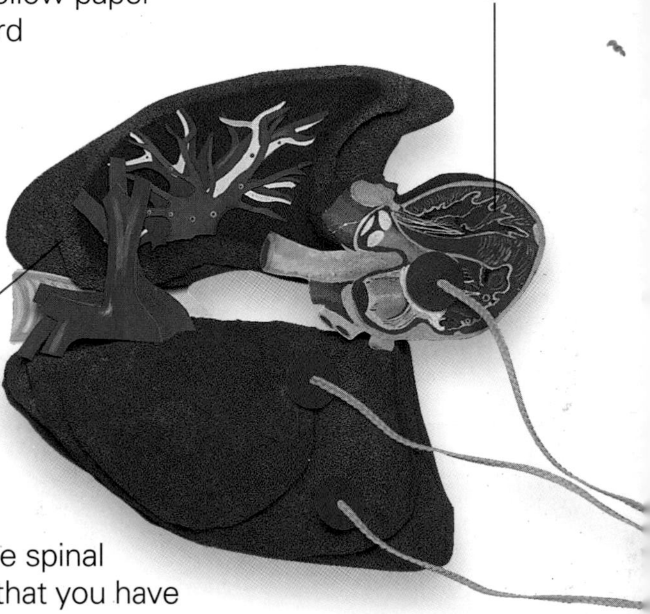

heart (p. 22)

lung (p. 24)

1 Take the spinal column that you have already made (see page 6).

2 Cut out 16 small disks and 3 larger oval shapes from yellow paper and 9 disks from red paper.

3 Cut 16 pieces of yellow cord.

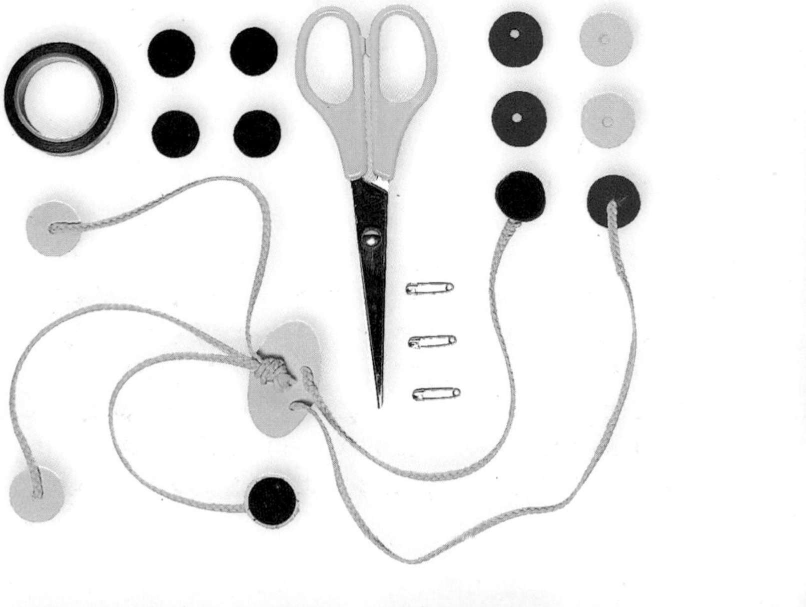

4 As you work through the book, make models of the body's organs and join them to the nervous system. Glue yellow cord to the red disks and attach the disks to the organs.

5 Thread the cord through the larger yellow disks, then knot it. These disks are like junctions, where nerves from several organs meet. Tape together the nerves from the heart and lungs.

6 Attach the remaining pieces of cord to the larger yellow disks as shown. Then stick the loose ends of the cords to the small yellow disks and glue these to the spine. The bones of the spine protect the delicate nerve endings.

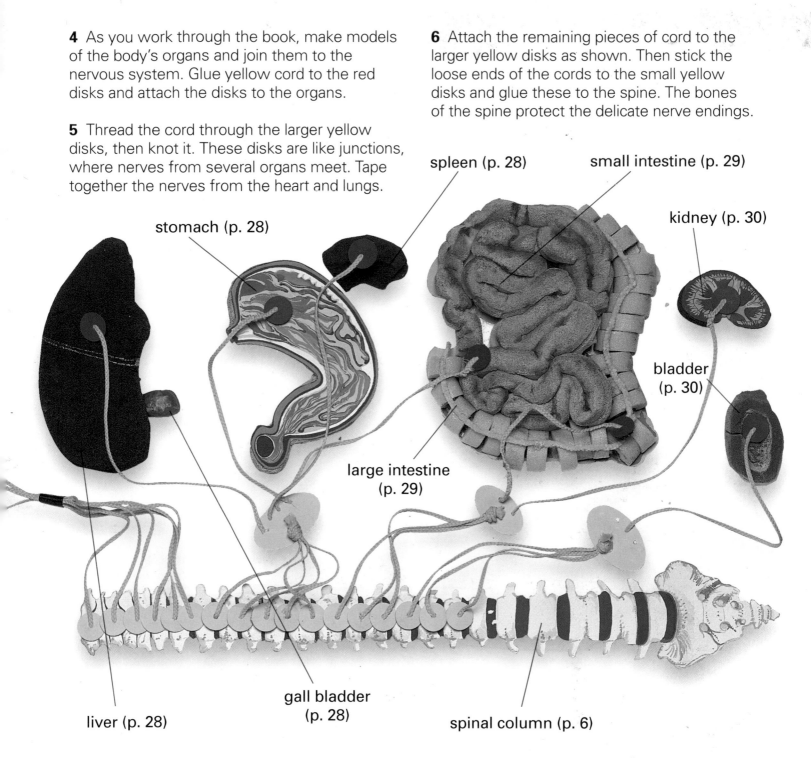

spleen (p. 28)

small intestine (p. 29)

kidney (p. 30)

stomach (p. 28)

bladder (p. 30)

large intestine (p. 29)

liver (p. 28)

gall bladder (p. 28)

spinal column (p. 6)

Sensory nerves
The nerves in your body constantly send messages about the outside world to your brain, which then sends back a response. For example, if you sip a cup of hot chocolate that is too hot, the nerves in your tongue send an urgent message to your brain. It then sends a message back along the nervous system to the muscles of your hand, telling them to put the cup down.

*Your muscles sometimes work without your brain thinking about them. The movements they make are called **reflex** actions and are controlled by the spinal cord alone, bypassing the brain. Try testing your reflexes. Sit in a chair with one leg crossed over the other. Ask a friend to tap your crossed leg just below the kneecap. What happens to this leg?*

Your body contains ten to twelve pints of blood, which carries oxygen and digested food all over your body and collects waste. It is pumped around by your heart. Blood helps your body to fight infection, and it controls how warm or cold you are by spreading heat as it circulates.

The blood transportation system

The red and blue yarn shows how blood is carried around the body in **blood vessels**. The arteries (shown in red) are the main highways of the blood system. They divide into smaller blood vessels. Tiny **capillaries** pass between the cells of the body, delivering oxygen from the lungs and carrying food to every part.

Waste products are carried away in capillaries, which gradually join up to make veins (shown by the blue yarn).

MAKE it WORK!

This model shows what blood is made of. It contains red cells, white cells, small fragments of cells called **platelets**, and a liquid called **plasma**, in which the other blood cells float. Whenever we cut ourselves, platelets surround the wound and make a fine net, called fibrin, which seals the wound.

You will need

glue	pieces of thin wire
a scouring pad	a foam base block
five table tennis balls	thick and thin sponges
red, yellow, and black paint	

1 Paint the foam base black. Cut circles from a thin sponge to make platelets. Push a piece of wire into each platelet and then into the base.

2 Next, make the red blood cells. Cut out six large ovals from the thick sponge and paint them red. Attach them to the base with pieces of wire.

3 Now make the white blood cells. Paint the table tennis balls and the scouring pad yellow. Shred the scouring pad. Tape a piece of wire to each ball, then cover it with some shredded scouring pad. Push the wires into the base.

4 Take the rest of the shredded scouring pad and spread it around the blood cells. This represents fibrin, which is made by the platelets.

fibrin

red blood cell
carries oxygen to all parts of the body

platelet
helps the blood to seal a wound by clotting

white blood cell
helps to fight infection

*When harmful bacteria enter your body and make you feel sick, white blood cells make **antibodies**. These attack the bacteria and stop them from multiplying. When you are immunized, you are injected with a mild form of the poison produced by disease-causing bacteria.*

White blood cells react immediately by making antibodies. Your body is now ready to fight the real disease.

Your heart is a muscle. Its job is to pump blood through blood vessels around your body. It has to repeat the same pumping action all your life, about once a second, to keep you alive. Blood containing oxygen is pumped through the left side of your heart to all parts of your body. When the oxygen has been used up, the blood is collected and sent back to the right side of your heart, and then to your lungs, where the blood is filled with oxygen again.

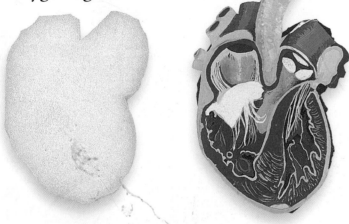

▲ Cut out pieces of sponge and cardboard, glue them together, and paint as shown. You will see that your model heart is divided into left and right sides, each with upper and lower chambers.

MAKE it WORK!
Make a pumping model to show how the four chambers in your heart work. Imagine how strong the muscle must be to repeat this action at least 60 times a minute!

You will need
four plastic bottles with screw-on tops
electrical tape   two plastic funnels
two bulldog clips   two pieces of plastic tubing
red and blue food coloring, tape, and
   modeling clay

1 Make small holes in the bottle tops. Cut two short pieces of plastic tubing and push each end of both tubes into a bottle top. Seal the holes around the tubes with red or blue modeling clay.

2 Make holes in the base of two of the plastic bottles and in the sides of the other two.

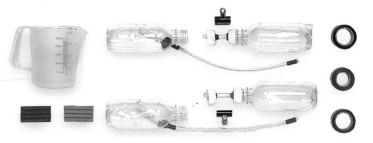

3 Thread two longer pieces of plastic tubing through the holes in the sides of the bottles. Push the tubes almost to the bottoms of the bottles. Seal the holes with modeling clay as before. Wrap red tape around the left-hand tube, and blue tape around the right-hand tube.

4 Now screw all four lids onto the bottles. Use electrical tape to join the bottles together in pairs, making sure that those with holes in the base are upside down at the top.

5 Dye two jugs of water, one with blue and one with red food coloring. Blood that contains oxygen is red. Blue water represents blood returning to the heart for more oxygen.

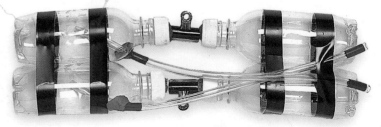

6 Attach bulldog clips to the tubes that connect the two bottles. These will do the same job as the heart's **valves**. They are like swinging doors that open only one way. Once the blood has passed from the heart's upper chamber, the valves close.

7 Using the funnels, carefully pour the red water into the bottle on the red side. Now pour blue water into the blue side. Open the bulldog clips to let the "blood" run through the tubes, then close them.

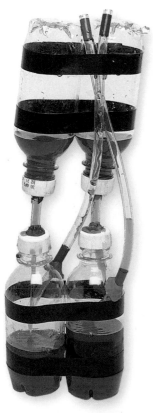

8 Squeeze the lower bottles. This action is similar to the pumping of the heart. See how quickly the blood spurts out of the tubes, ready to be pumped all around the body.

Test your own, or a friend's, heartbeat. Find your pulse on the inside of your wrist or at the side of your neck. When you feel it beating under your fingers, count how many beats you can feel in a minute. Take your pulse before and after doing some exercise. You will notice a big difference!

Your lungs have a very important job to do: They must absorb as much oxygen as possible from the air. We all need oxygen and also some carbon dioxide to keep us alive. When you breathe in, air is taken into your lungs. Oxygen is absorbed into the blood and is carried all over your body through your blood vessels. Your body combines oxygen with the food you eat so that it can produce energy.

MAKE it WORK!
Did you know that adults' lungs hold about ten pints of air? Find out your own lung capacity, or how much air your lungs can hold, by doing this simple experiment.

3 Place the palm of your hand over the open end of the bottle. Quickly turn it upside down and plunge it into the bowl. When you remove your hand, the water will stay in the bottle.

4 Tape the straws together. Slide one end under the bottle. Take a deep breath, and blow out into the other end of the straw.

5 Increased air pressure forces the water out of the bottle. Using your scale, measure the amount of air at the top of the bottle. This is your lung capacity. Now run in place for one minute, and try doing the experiment again. Does exercise affect your lung capacity?

You will need

a large bowl
a measuring cup
insulating tape

a plastic bottle
two straws

1 Fill the bowl with water. Cut the top off the plastic bottle. Fill the measuring cup with water, and note down how much it holds.

2 Pour this water into the bottle. Using the tape, mark a scale (use 8-10 sections) up the side of the bottle.

A newborn baby's lungs are pink. As you get older, your lungs get blacker because of the polluted air you breathe. Lungs are very sensitive to the quality of air, so your body tries to protect them in all sorts of ways. Dry air is moistened by mucus in the nose as you breathe in. If the air is too cold, blood vessels in the nose will heat it up. Hairs in the nose trap particles of dust and dirt in the air before they reach your lungs.

MAKE it WORK!

The lungs are not muscles. They expand when they are filled with air because of the action of the diaphragm, a flat muscle at the base of the ribs, and the chest wall. This experiment shows you how your diaphragm allows your lungs to breathe. The plastic bottle represents your chest, the straw is your throat, the yellow balloon is your diaphragm, and the blue balloon is your lungs. As your diaphragm stretches and contracts, it inflates and deflates your lungs.

You will need

modeling clay   a yellow balloon
a blue balloon   a straw
two rubber bands
a small strip of wood
the upper half of a plastic bottle with lid

1 Cut the wood to fit the width of the bottle exactly. Glue it inside the cut end of the bottle.

2 Secure the yellow balloon over the open end of the bottle with a rubber band.

3 Make a small hole in the bottle top. Push the straw through. Attach the blue balloon to the end of the straw with a rubber band. Seal the hole with modeling clay.

4 Screw the top back on the bottle with the blue balloon inside.

5 Stretch the yellow balloon downward. This reduces the air pressure inside the bottle. More air is sucked in through the straw to fill the space, which inflates the blue balloon (your lungs).

6 Now push in the yellow balloon to make the "diaphragm" contract. The air pressure inside the bottle increases and forces air out through the straw. The blue balloon goes down. This is what happens when you breathe out.

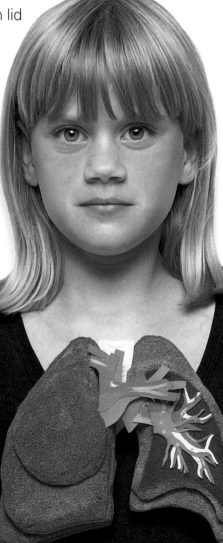

▶ Make a pair of lungs by cutting out these foam shapes. Paint them as shown. The right-hand lung is a cross section.

◀ Air passes down the branching tubes inside the lungs. It reaches air sacs, called **alveoli**. From here, the oxygen is passed into the blood.

You begin **digesting** your food as soon as you put it in your mouth. This is just the start of its long journey. It will take about two days for the food to pass all the way through your digestive system. During this journey, your body will break the food down until it has taken out the **nutrients** it needs.

You will need

a block of Styrofoam
red, blue, and green wires
red, blue, and green straws
a felt-tip pen
acrylic paint
a craft file
sandpaper

1 Draw the molar on the Styrofoam. Molars are large teeth at the back of the mouth, used for grinding food.

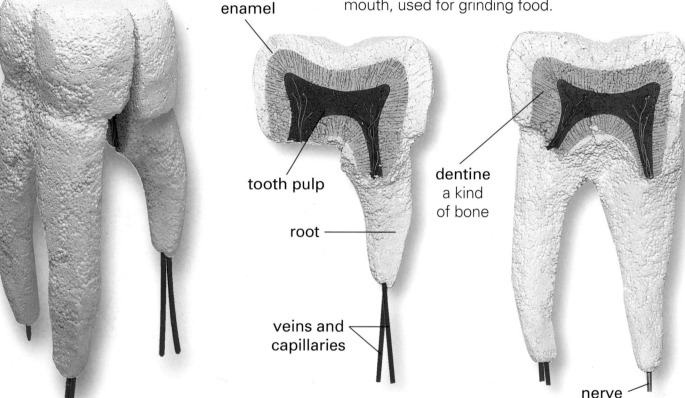

enamel

tooth pulp

root

veins and capillaries

dentine
a kind
of bone

nerve

MAKE it WORK!

Your teeth are used in the first stage of your digestion. They chop, shred, and grind up food in your mouth. Glands under your tongue make a liquid called **saliva**, which moistens the food and begins to break it down. When you have finished chewing your food, your tongue moves it to the back of your mouth. With one swallow your food starts its journey. Make a model molar and see what a tooth is like inside.

2 Carefully carve out the three roots. About a quarter of the way down the tooth, shape a ridge. Above this ridge, or gumline, the tooth is visible. Shape a ridge in the top of the tooth. Smooth down the Styrofoam with sandpaper.

3 Now cut your molar in half to reveal the inside of the tooth. Paint it as shown. The enamel on the visible part of the tooth is whiter than the roots deep inside the gum.

4 Take the red and blue straws, which represent the capillaries and veins. Push them into the root of the tooth. Then take the blue and red wires and twist them around in the pulp cavity as shown. This is the soft center of the tooth.

5 Do the same with the green straw and wire. This represents the tooth's nerve. If your tooth enamel decays, it can expose the nerve, which will give you toothache.

Human beings can eat meat as well as vegetables, so we have teeth to suit both these kinds of food. At the front of our mouths, we have sharp, pointed teeth, which we use for tearing and shredding meat. Our large back teeth are used to grind vegetables. Animals such as cows only have grinding teeth because they eat only grass.

Bacteria live in your mouth because it is dark, warm, and moist. They feed on sugars in your food and produce acids that can harm your teeth.

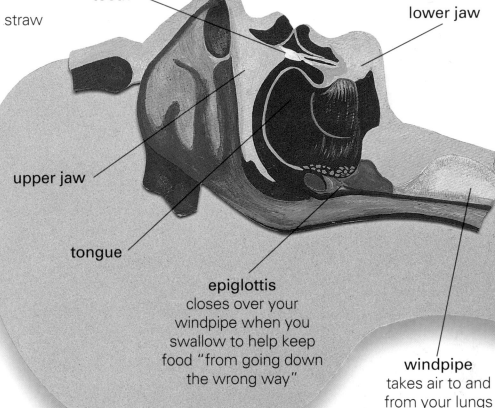

tooth

lower jaw

upper jaw

tongue

epiglottis
closes over your windpipe when you swallow to help keep food "from going down the wrong way"

windpipe
takes air to and from your lungs when you breathe

It is very important to brush your teeth as often as possible, because brushing is the only way to fight the germs that lurk between them and along your gums.

MAKE it WORK!
Make this model head to find out what the inside of your nose, mouth, and throat look like. Use the labels to help you identify each part.

Sometimes your food "goes down the wrong way." This means that some food has gotten into your windpipe. If this happens, you start to choke. Air rushes up your windpipe very fast, pushing the food back into your mouth.

A good diet
What you eat and drink provides your body with the things it needs to keep healthy. A balanced diet provides important vitamins and minerals. Proteins, found in meat, fish, eggs, milk, cheese, and nuts, help you to grow. Carbohydrates, found in pasta, bread, sugar, and potatoes, give you energy. Fiber, found in fruit, vegetables, and whole grains, cannot easily be broken down. It helps to keep your digestive system working properly and passes out of your body as waste.

To support overlapping organs on your model, cut small squares of foam and paint them pink. Remember that the body does not have these!

1 Paint a cardboard base for your digestive system.

2 Cut out foam shapes for the liver, spleen, and stomach, and paint them.

esophagus
the tube that leads from the mouth to the stomach; pushes food down by muscular movements

stomach
makes acidic digestive juices that pour on food and begin to break down protein; food stays in the stomach for about two hours

liver
receives nutrients from the blood, storing some and passing others on; also filters out poisons and uses energy from food to heat the blood

gall bladder (tucked underneath liver) stores bile, which helps to break down fats and turn them into chemicals, which can be absorbed through the intestine wall

spleen
helps fight infection, stores blood, and removes worn-out red cells from blood

You will need
foam or sponge
tube insulation
modeling clay
a felt-tip pen
acrylic paint
green wire
cardboard
Velcro

3 Make a cone out of modeling clay for the gall bladder and paint it dark green. Push both green wires into the point of the cone and attach them at the other end to the liver.

4 Cut a gray cardboard base for the small intestine. Thread wire through a long strip of foam. Bend it to shape, paint it pink, and glue it in place.

5 For the large intestine, cut the tube insulation in half lengthwise, slice it up, and glue the u-shaped pieces around the small intestine.

6 Stick the organs to the body base using Velcro disks.

large intestine
receives remains of food from the small intestine; waste products (including fiber, the part of food that is not digested) move down to the end of the intestine

rectum
the end of the large intestine; waste passes out through here when you empty your bowels

small intestine
receives digested food from the stomach; chemicals from the food are absorbed into the bloodstream through the intestine wall

appendix
a dead end; not used by humans, but helps certain animals to digest grass

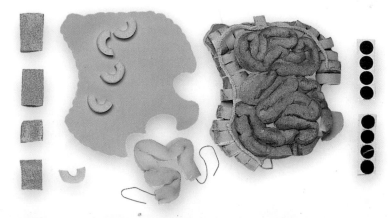

If you eat too much food, or any food that is bad, your body has a very effective way of getting rid of it. The muscles of your stomach wall squeeze in and force the food back up your esophagus and out of your body. This is called vomiting or throwing up.

Water is vital to your body. Seventy percent of your body weight is water. Water carries important chemicals, such as nutrients and heat, around your body. You absorb it when you eat, drink, and breathe. You lose it when you sweat or go to the toilet.

kidney

ureter
tubes carrying urine
from kidneys to
bladder

nerves

blood vessels

bladder

Your kidneys work very efficiently to filter unwanted water and waste products from your blood. From these they make **urine**, a liquid that flushes waste out of the body. They process 33 gallons of water a day.

MAKE it WORK!
Make a model of your purification system. It includes your kidneys, two small, bean-shaped organs found behind your waist. Tubes join them to your bladder, where urine is stored.

You will need
blue and red wire
sponge or foam
pipe cleaners
cardboard

1 Cut foam shapes for the kidneys and bladder and a matching cardboard shape for the kidney in cross section. Paint them as shown.

2 Cut out cardboard blood vessels and paint them blue and red. These blood vessels supply blood to the kidneys.

3 Attach the red and blue wires and pipe cleaners as shown. The wires are the nerves leading to and from your bladder. The pipe cleaners are the tubes that carry urine.

MAKE it WORK!

When blood passes through them, the kidneys act like a very fine sieve, filtering out waste products and purifying the blood. You can see how the kidneys work by doing this simple filtering experiment.

You will need

pieces of Styrofoam
three strips of wood
a plastic bottle
food coloring
sand or soil

a measuring cup
a glass tumbler
fine netting
tape

3 Make three filters by taping the netting to the bottle sections. Make one filter with just one piece of net, the second with three pieces of net, and the third with six pieces of net.

4 Glue the three strips of wood to the edge of the filters, as shown, so that they are freestanding.

5 Fill a measuring cup with water. Then add food coloring (which contains very fine particles), sand or soil, and chunks of Styrofoam. These represent the different waste products in the blood when it arrives in the kidneys.

1 Ask an adult to help you slice three sections from the bottle.

2 Cut out ten circles of netting. They should be slightly larger than the bottle sections.

6 Pour the water through the filters and watch what happens. Everything except the finest food coloring particles is caught by the filters.

Sometimes, because of an accident or disease, the kidneys fail and cannot clean the blood. A special machine can be used to do their job. Blood is taken from an artery in the arm and passed through the machine, where it is cleaned and returned to the body. This is called dialysis. The blood has to pass through the machine 20 times before it is thoroughly cleaned. Patients have to spend two 12-hour sessions on the machine every week.

Your brain is the control center of your body. It runs all your body's functions and movements. It is also responsible for thoughts, memories, and emotions.

Although it is quite small, your brain contains more than 100,000 nerve cells. It uses up one-fifth of your body's energy, so it needs a constant supply of oxygen.

1 Ask an adult to help you cut down the plastic ball so that it makes a neatly-fitting skullcap. This is the cortex, or outer layer of the brain.

2 Copy all the shapes shown on different colored paper (see tip on page 8). These represent the different parts of the body that the brain controls.

MAKE it WORK!
Each part of the brain takes care of a different body function. Make your own skullcap and plot which parts of your brain control which actions.

You will need
glue	
pipe cleaners	colored paper
half a plastic ball	paper fasteners

3 Bend the pipe cleaners in half and twist them. Glue a cardboard shape to the bent end of each.

4 Make eight holes in the cap, following the photograph opposite. Push the open ends of each pipe cleaner through the right hole and bend the ends to hold it in position. Put on your skullcap to see exactly how your mind works!

movements
all your main muscular movements are controlled from here

speech
this part of your brain controls your voice box and the muscles of your mouth

touching
your brain receives signals from your skin here

hands
all your hand movements are controlled from here

hearing
messages from your ears are dealt with in this part of the brain

focus
this is where your brain makes pictures out of the messages received from your eyes

balance
this part of your brain makes sure you don't fall over!

eye muscles
this part of your brain controls the muscles around your eyes

The cortex of your brain is pinkish-gray (it is known as "gray matter"). It has the texture of custard.

The brain stem is the part of your brain nearest to your spinal cord. It acts like an automatic pilot. It runs all your body's main systems; for example, your digestion and circulation, and also your heart and lungs.

Everything you know is stored in your brain. As time passes, your brain processes everything that happens to you. Much of this information is stored in your short-term memory, and you will forget it quickly. For example, your memory of the pictures on the previous page will soon fade. Other experiences you remember for much longer, because they are stored in your long-term memory. Everything you remember helps you to learn.

MAKE it WORK!

The brain helps us to understand what we see by remembering things we have seen before. But sometimes it can be fooled. This is known as an optical illusion. Make these illusions and confuse your friends!

You will need

thin black cardboard
thin colored cardboard
a felt-tip pen

a ruler
scissors

▲ Using the ruler, cut two straight strips of dark colored cardboard. Draw the pattern of straight lines on light cardboard and position the dark strips over it as shown. Do the dark lines look straight? The pattern of lines underneath has tricked your brain, making the dark strips look curved.

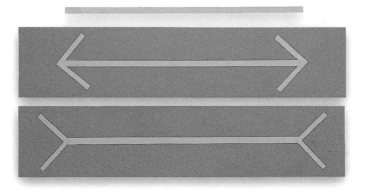

▲ Now cut out the two simple arrow shapes from light cardboard, as shown. Make sure that the center lines are the same length. You will see that the arrowheads create an illusion. They make the center lines look shorter and longer than they really are.

▲ Trace the outline of the left-hand side of the candlestick on colored paper. Fold the paper in half and cut along the line. Unfold the paper and glue the candlestick to the center of the black cardboard. As well as the candlestick, can you also see two faces looking at each other.

▶ Cut this shape from colored cardboard. Is it a duck or a rabbit? Your brain can see only one image at a time.

MAKE it WORK!

This game is a good way to test your short-term memory. Try playing it with a friend and see how many objects each of you can remember. Can you find any way of helping your brain to memorize the objects more easily?

You will need

assorted everyday objects   pencil and paper
a tray or drawer
a cloth

2 Show the objects on the tray to a friend. Ask your friend to look at them for about a minute and try to memorize them, then cover the tray.

3 Give your friend a few moments to think, then see how many of the objects he or she can remember. Write them down and check them against the objects on the tray. Now try swapping places. Ask your friend to find a new set of objects and see how many of them you can remember.

1 Choose about 20 different small objects from around the house. Try to make sure that they are not related to each other in any way (for example, do not choose objects that could all be found in your school desk). Lay everything out on the tray.

Ways to remember

The brain works better if you organize the things you are trying to remember. You could do this by putting them in alphabetical order, arranging them by color, or even making up a story about them. Maybe you will find that your brain works better in pictures. You can take a number of different objects and imagine them in a crazy picture. Try playing the game using these ways of remembering and see whether you can improve your score.

Most people cannot remember a series of more than nine numbers. Telephone numbers are only seven digits long (if you don't count the area code). If phone numbers were longer, people would have trouble remembering them!

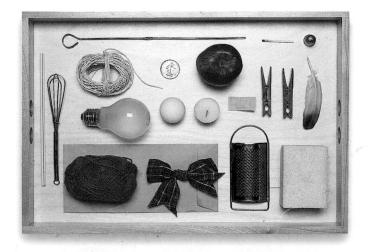

There are five main senses – sight, hearing, touch, smell, and taste. They send vital information to your brain about the world around you. Your eyes are the sense organs that receive information in the form of light rays bouncing off everything you see. Your eyes turn these rays into messages that your brain can understand.

You will need

red and blue wire	a flashlight
an old plastic ball	Scotch tape
a magnifying glass	acrylic paint
thick and thin dowels	thin cardboard
a clear plastic bottle	corrugated cardboard

1 Ask an adult to help you cut the ball in half, trim the flat base from the plastic bottle, and cut short pieces of thick and thin dowel in half lengthwise with a sharp knife or saw.

The eye is shaped like a ball and contains a jellylike fluid. It has a clear covering (the cornea) at the front. The colored part of the eye is called the iris; it has a small hole at its center (the pupil) through which light enters. The lens is behind the pupil and it focuses light on the retina, a special lining at the back of the eyeball. The retina detects the light rays and turns them into messages that go to the brain along the optic nerve.

MAKE it WORK!

Make this model eye and see for yourself how your eyes are your windows to the world!

2 Paint the inside of one half of the ball red, with lighter red and blue veins. This represents the retina.

3 Cut out the cardboard shapes and paint them as shown. Glue them together, placing the red muscles at the top and bottom. Tape the cardboard shape around the cut edge of the ball.

4 Twist the blue and red wires together, and stick one end inside the ball, as shown. Glue the dowels together, paint them, then stick them in position on the cardboard. This is the optic nerve, joining the eye to the brain.

5 Slot the magnifying glass and bottle base into position in the cardboard, as shown. They represent the lens and the cornea.

Your pupils control the amount of light entering your eyes. Look at yourself in a mirror in a dimly lit room. Your pupils, the black spots in the middle of your eyes, will be quite large. This helps them to let in as much light as possible so that you can see the room. Now turn on the light and notice how quickly your pupils react to the light by getting smaller.

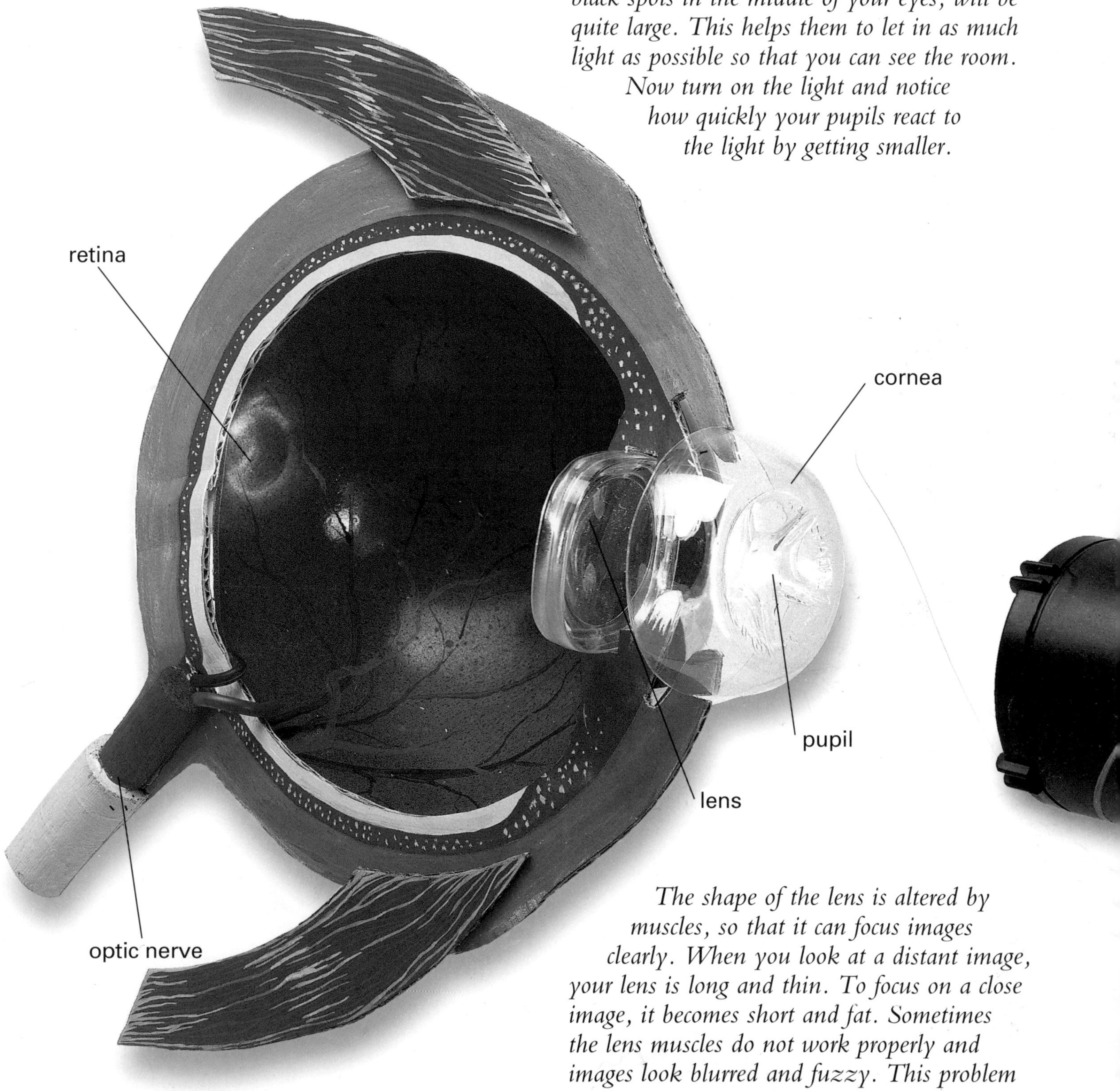

retina

cornea

pupil

lens

optic nerve

6 Shine the flashlight through the cornea. You can see how the lens focuses light on the retina.

The shape of the lens is altered by muscles, so that it can focus images clearly. When you look at a distant image, your lens is long and thin. To focus on a close image, it becomes short and fat. Sometimes the lens muscles do not work properly and images look blurred and fuzzy. This problem is helped by wearing more lenses, such as glasses or contact lenses, to correct the focus.

Your sense of smell helps you to recognize things at a distance, while your sense of taste detects the flavors of food and drinks. You use both senses to check that food is fresh and will not harm you. Taste buds on your tongue's surface detect how salty, sweet, sour, or bitter food is when it is mixed with saliva. Tiny hairs inside your nose pick up scent particles in the air and tell you about the flavor of food, too. If you have a stuffy nose, you usually lose most of your sense of taste.

▼ Blindfold your friend. First, put a few drops of each liquid on his or her tongue, and see if your friend can recognize whether it is bitter, sweet, sour, or salty. Write down the answers.

Certain parts of your tongue are more sensitive to some foods than others, because different taste buds detect different flavors. In general, the sweet and salty taste buds are near the front of the tongue. Sour and bitter taste buds are at the back and sides.

Experiment by putting the liquids on different parts of your friend's tongue. Note down his or her guesses and see if he or she is right.

MAKE it WORK!
How good is your sense of taste? Wine tasters can tell the difference between many different flavors. Can you recognize the four main flavors – bitter, sweet, sour, and salty – when you are blindfolded?

You will need
a blindfold   a teaspoon
water for rinsing the teaspoon between tests
samples of sweet, salty, sour, and bitter liquids, for example, sugar in water, salt in water, lemon juice in water, and black coffee

Our food and drink has many variations on sweet, salty, sour, and bitter tastes. We can tell flavors apart from the smell of the things we eat; without the sense of smell, it can be difficult to tell foods apart. Experiment with this by asking your friend to hold his or her nose. Give your friend a piece of apple and a piece of onion to eat. Can your friend tell what he or she is eating?

Your tongue isn't just used for tasting. It moves food around so your teeth can chew it, and it pushes the food to the back of your mouth so you can swallow it.

MAKE it WORK!

Make a gigantic model tongue in Styrofoam, and find out exactly where the different types of taste buds are found.

1 Using the craft file, cut out the Styrofoam in the shape shown. Paint the tongue pink.

2 Cut out the bubble wrap in the shape of the tongue and paint it pink. Position it on to the tongue model.

You will need
thumb tacks in four different colors
a sheet of bubble wrap
acrylic paint
Styrofoam
a craft file
glue

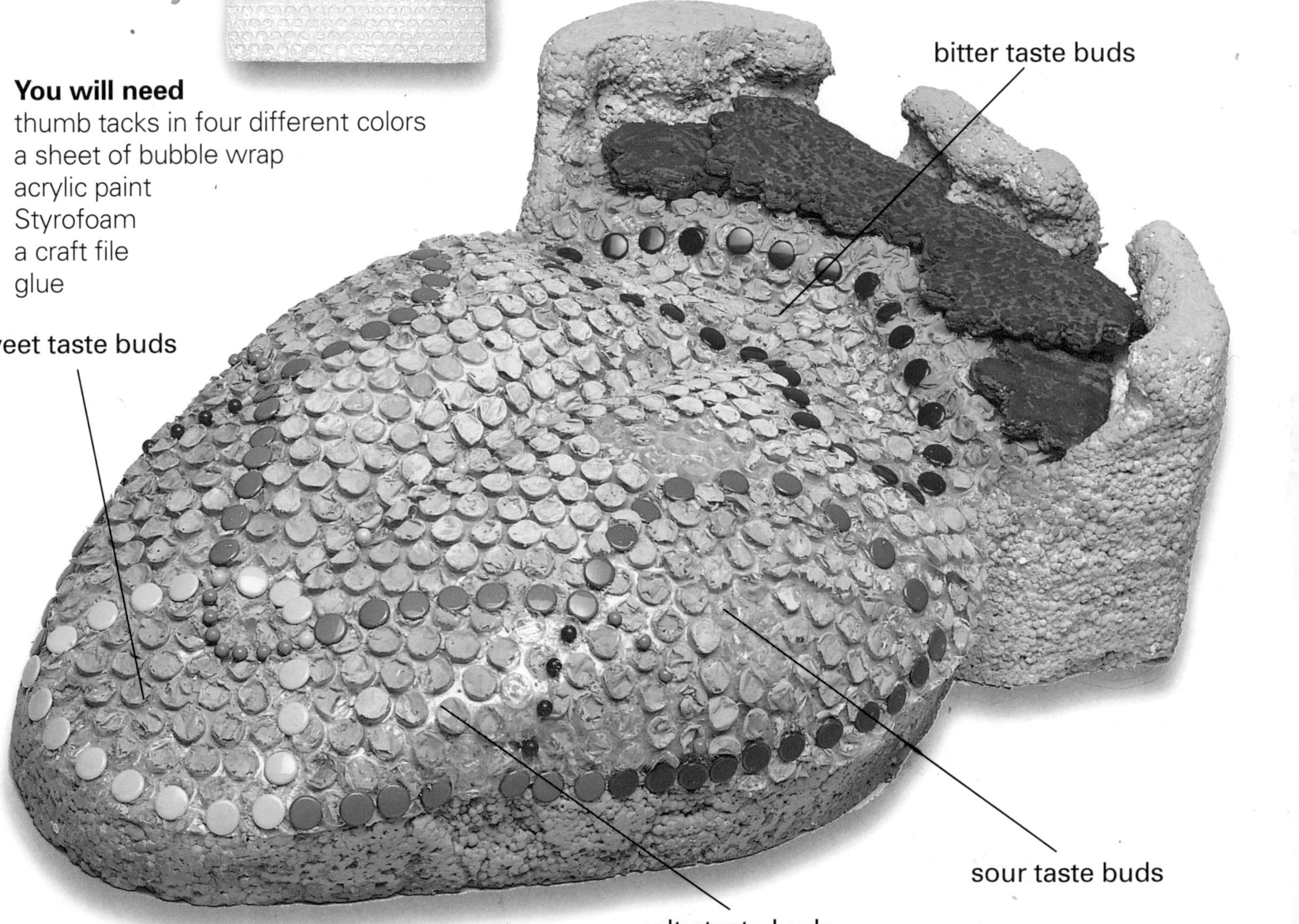

bitter taste buds

sweet taste buds

sour taste buds

salty taste buds

Scent particles are chemicals that float around in the air we breathe. Humans can recognize about 3,000 separate smelly chemicals, and many more smells that are combinations of these.

3 Stick the different colored thumb tacks through the bubble wrap and into the tongue, as shown. These show where the sweet, salty, sour, and bitter taste buds are located.

Nerve endings all over your skin give you a sense of touch. They react to heat and cold, texture, pressure, and pain. Your sense of hearing can alert you to things you may not have seen, or that are out of reach. It also helps you to communicate with other people.

1 Put the first finger of your left hand into the hot water, and the first finger of your right hand into the cold water.

2 Wait for about a minute then, one at a time, dip each finger into the warm water.

3 The finger from the hot water feels cold, because it senses a drop in temperature. The finger from the cold water will feel warm, because it senses a temperature increase.

MAKE it WORK!

Test how your skin reacts to heat and cold and changes in temperature by doing this simple experiment. Not all parts of your skin have the same number of nerves. Fingertips, toes, and lips are the most sensitive parts of the body.

You will need

a glass of warm water   a glass of cold water
a glass of hot tap water

Blind people are able to read using a system called Braille. Patterns of raised bumps, representing letters and words, are made on the page. The blind person can read what is written by touching the bumps with his or her fingertips, which can become especially sensitive. This system of writing was invented in 1824 by a Frenchman, Louis Braille, who became blind at the age of three.

MAKE it WORK!
Try the blindfold test and see how much you can find out using only your sense of touch.

You will need
a large cardboard box
assorted objects
a large cloth

1 Turn the box on its side, and make a hole in the base large enough to put your hands through. Drape the cloth over the box.

2 Place various objects in the box. Try to choose things that feel different. For example, a spoon is hard and metallic, yarn is soft, a brush is bristly.

3 Try the touch test on a friend. When your friend puts his or her hands through the slot, he or she will not be able to see the objects. Ask your friend to describe what he or she is touching.

Hearing
Sounds are made by air vibrating. Your ears act as sound collectors, picking up these vibrations and trapping them in your outer ear. From here, the sounds pass down to your eardrum, which is a very thin piece of skin separating your outer ear from your middle ear. The eardrum vibrates in turn, passing the sound on to three small bones in your middle ear. One of these, the tiny stirrup bone, is about the size of a grain of rice. The vibrations are then passed into the fluid inside your inner ear, deep inside your skull. From here they are converted into electrical signals and passed on to your brain.

Is it soft? Is it rough? Is it cold and hard like metal? What shape is it? Can he or she guess what the object is? Now ask your friend to place some different objects in the box. How many of these can you identify?

The brain is able to separate sounds into those you want to hear and background noises. You can often hear your friend talking even though a huge truck is thundering past.

The nucleus of every cell in your body contains a set of coded instructions called genes, which are made from a special chemical called DNA. Each cell contains thousands of genes that affect your looks, character, and abilities.

When a new life begins, a set of genes from the mother and a set from the father are brought together in one cell. As new cells grow, the pattern from the parents' genes is repeated. This is called heredity. You are a combination of your parents' genes. If their genes are different, you will inherit the stronger, or dominant, gene. For example, if you inherit genes for both brown and blue eyes, you will probably have brown eyes, because the brown-eye gene is dominant.

MAKE it WORK!
How many characteristics do you share with the rest of your family? You are not exactly like them. With every generation, new sets of genes are introduced into a family. Play the generation game and see for yourself the vast number of variations that are possible.

1 Using modeling clay (which you can then paint), make two shapes, such as a ball and a cube. These will represent the first generation of your family.

2 Now find out what happens as these shapes combine to make new ones in the next generation.

3 Introduce a different shape to the second generation. How will it affect the third? One generation may produce a set of identical twins. The fertilized egg has divided to make two babies who share exactly the same genes.

Sometimes genes contain instructions that can be harmful. Many serious illnesses are hereditary. Hemophilia (which stops your blood from clotting if you are wounded) is passed on by mothers, who rarely suffer from the disease themselves, to their sons.

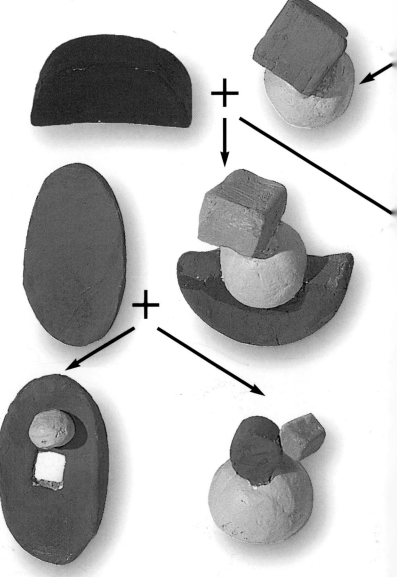

Now that you have discovered how many variations are possible through the generations of a family, make a real family tree and see how many similarities you can find. Use photographs of your own family or a friend's family, if possible. They will help you to recognize features that have been passed on through the generations.

Try to start your family tree with all four grandparents. Line up their names and pictures at the top. Then add their children underneath, along with each child's husband or wife. This line will include your own or your friend's parents, aunts, and uncles. The next line down will be your generation, and includes brothers, sisters, and cousins. How many family members share characteristics?

You'll be amazed by what you can inherit from your parents. Apart from obvious things like the shape of your face and features and your height, some very odd things are passed on in the genes. Double-jointed thumbs are hereditary. So is the ability to roll your tongue up at the edges.

Your body is an efficient, smooth-running machine. By now, you will have seen that it contains a number of different systems, each with its own job to do. These systems keep your body running from day to day. Food and oxygen are taken in, carried in your blood, and used as a source of energy. Your body gets rid of waste products efficiently. Messages are carried back and forth between your brain and the outside world. But your body also has to deal with problems. It is the job of your defense, or **immune**, system to fight infection and repair your body when things go wrong.

▶ Now that you have made all your main body systems, you can lay them out and see how they work together.

Skin
The skin helps to control the body's temperature. It protects the organs of the body, and is also the organ of touch.

Skeleton
The 206 bones of the body provide a framework and protect important organs. Red blood cells are made in the bone marrow.

Muscles
The muscles are responsible for moving the body. Involuntary muscles also keep other body systems (such as the digestive system) running smoothly.

Nervous system
This system consists of the brain, spinal cord, nerves, and sense organs. Nerves carry messages to and from the brain. The nervous system controls all the body's activities.

Blood
The blood system consists of the heart, blood, and blood vessels. Blood transports oxygen and nutrients to the cells and takes away waste products. White blood cells also protect you from disease.

Breathing
The lungs are responsible for taking in the oxygen from the air you breathe and passing it into your blood.

Digestion
This system is one long tube through which food passes. It starts at your mouth and ends at your rectum. Organs such as the liver, gall bladder, and pancreas help to break the food down and extract nutrients from it.

Purification
Your kidneys purify the blood and get rid of waste.

Things that go wrong

When you think how much your body has to do, it seems amazing that it runs so smoothly. When things do go wrong, your body will try its best to fix them.

Bacteria are tiny living organisms. They live all around us and are often harmless. Some bacteria, however, reproduce very rapidly inside your body and can make you feel sick because they produce poisons. Infected wounds, food poisoning, and tonsillitis are all examples of illnesses caused by bacteria.

A bad fall or accident can sometimes break or fracture bones in your body. A broken bone can be "set" by being held back in its correct position by a plaster cast. The bone on either side of the break then knits together, repairing the damage. An accident may also pull a joint out of place, or **dislocate** it. A doctor can move the bones back into the correct position.

Although many things can go wrong with a complicated machine like the human body, modern medicine can correct a lot of them. Over the centuries, medicine has made great progress. The twentieth century in particular has seen many important advances and people now live longer than in the past. Scientists are still working to find cures for diseases such as AIDS and cancer, and exciting new discoveries about the body are still being made.

Viruses are tiny **organisms** that invade the body's cells. Once they are inside a cell, they change it into a mini-factory that produces more and more viruses. Eventually the cell bursts and dies, releasing the new viruses into the body.

Viruses cause a huge range of diseases – from the common cold to influenza, chicken pox, and measles. The body fights viruses by producing antibodies in the white blood cells – often this process can make you feel sick, too.

As a human body grows older, its systems begin to slow down. Cells renew themselves more slowly, the skin wrinkles, and muscles become looser. The senses are less sharp, and the body finds it harder to fight disease. But these signs of aging go hand in hand with gaining a lifetime of knowledge and experience, which can be a pleasure.

Alveoli Tiny sacs in the lungs where gas is exchanged. Oxygen is collected and absorbed into the blood. Carbon dioxide is removed from the blood to the lungs where it is exhaled.

Antibodies Substances in your blood that destroy the harmful bacteria and viruses.

Blood vessels The tubes, such as veins and arteries, through which blood circulates.

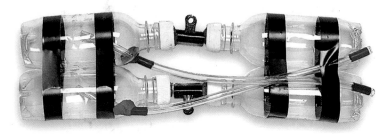

Capillary A tiny blood vessel that links larger ones and carries blood to and from your cells.

Cell The basic building blocks that make up your body. Each cell has a center, or nucleus, which contains the instructions it needs to do its job.

Chemicals Substances from which all things are made. There are many different chemicals in the human body.

Chromosome The nucleus of every cell contains structures called chromosomes, which carry genes. The genes control all the characteristics we inherit from our parents.

Digesting The action of breaking down food into chemicals that your body can absorb and can send to your cells to produce energy.

Dislocate A joint is dislocated when a bone is pushed out of place so the joint does not work.

Evaporate To change from a liquid to a gas; for example, water to steam.

Follicle A small pocket in your skin. Each hair on your body grows out of its own follicle.

Gland A cell or organ that either makes chemicals for your body to use or helps to remove waste products from your body. For example, sweat glands remove water, passing sweat out onto the surface of your skin.

Hereditary Transmitted from parent to child through the genes.

Immune Your immune system helps your body to fight disease and infection. When you have successfully fought off certain diseases, such as mumps, you become immune. Your body will be able to resist the disease if it attacks again.

Involuntary Describes the parts of your body that work without your having to think about them.

Joint The place where two bones meet. There are many different types of joints that allow your body to move in a variety of ways.

Keratin A hard substance made in the cells of your hair, skin, and nails.

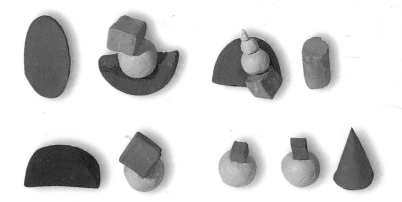

Ligament A tough, elastic band of tissue that holds bones together at a joint.

Marrow A soft, jellylike substance found inside most bones, where red blood cells and some white blood cells are made.

Melanin A colored substance in your skin that darkens it and protects it against the sun's harmful rays.

Metacarpal A bone that connects your finger or thumb to your wrist.

Muscle Muscles are made from strong, elastic tissue. They move the parts of your body.

Nutrient A chemical that your body extracts from food to give it energy to grow and work.

Organ A group of tissues that form a shape and work together to do a particular job in the body; for example, the heart or liver.

Organism A living thing.

Plasma The liquid part of your blood in which red and white blood cells and platelets float.

Platelet A minute particle in the blood. When you cut your skin, platelets surround the wound and make a fine net, or clot, which stops the bleeding.

Pore A tiny opening in the surface of the skin through which substances, such as sweat, pass.

Reflex An automatic response in your body, such as blinking or jerking your knee. You cannot stop a reflex by thinking about it.

Saliva A liquid produced by glands in your mouth. It moistens food, making it easier to swallow, and begins the chemical process of digestion by helping to break food down.

Sense The main senses are sight, smell, hearing, taste, and touch. They help you to find out about the world around you. Your brain receives messages from your sense organs: your eyes, nose, ears, tongue, and skin.

Skeletal Attached to the skeleton. Skeletal muscles move your bones and are responsible for body movements that you have to think about, such as walking.

Skeleton The bony framework that supports your body and protects delicate organs such as your heart and brain.

Species A group of plants or animals whose members share the same characteristics and can breed together successfully.

Tendon Special tissue that attaches your muscles to your bones.

Tissue A collection of cells, usually of the same type, that work together to make up a part of the body. For example, the skin is a type of tissue made up of many cells.

Urine A liquid made up of waste water and chemicals from the blood. It is made in the kidneys, passed down to the bladder, and then leaves your body via a tube called the urethra.

Valve Your veins and heart contain valves to keep blood from flowing backward. They open in one direction only. When blood has passed through them, they flap shut like swinging doors.